Mount Assiniboine

CONTENTS

Waterton Lakes National Park

WATERTON

In the complex environment of Waterton Lakes National Park, mountains rise abruptly from the prairies. The history of these mountains is fascinating, as they are said to be upside-down. During their formation, older sediment came to rest on top of much younger shales, leaving exposed some of North America's oldest rock.

Part of the upper lake lies in Glacier National Park, Montana. Thus, in the interest of maintaining good relations between Canada and the United States, the United Nations declared Waterton an International Peace Park.

Red Rock Canyon

Peter Lougheed Provincial Park

KANANASKIS

Kananaskis Country contains three provincial parks, and is thus a popular destination of Calgarians and Bow Valley residents alike. Because of its accessibility, K-Country makes possible an impulsive camping trip or back country ski tour. In the summer months, its magnificent golf course provides city-dwellers with a much-needed escape from the drudgery of the urban workplace.

Kananaskis is replete with some of the Rockies' more timid species of wildlife. Wolf tracks can be seen on cross-country ski trails in the winter, and sightings of moose are common.

Kananaskis Country Golf Course

Three Sisters

CANMORE

The Three Sisters are the signature mountains of this lovely alpine town. Since 1988, when Canmore hosted the Winter Olympic Games, the beauty of the area has drawn international attention. The Canmore Nordic Centre is a world-class facility featuring 56 km of cross-country ski trails which serve as mountain bike routes in the summer.

Canmore is also known for its unique artist community. A number of interesting galleries and shops display the ceramics, paintings, jewelry and sculptures of local craftspeople.

Elk

Mount Rundle and Vermilion Lakes

BANFF

Aside from its spectacular setting in the heart of the Canadian Rockies, Banff is the cultural nexus of the Bow Valley. Above the townsite is the Banff Centre, where some of the world's most talented artists, dancers and musicians convene.

The art and cultures of the Bow Valley's first inhabitants are displayed at the Luxton Museum and the Indian Trading Post. Their history in the Banff area, as well as that of early European mountaineers, is explored in the beautiful displays and archives of the Whyte Museum of the Canadian Rockies.

Bear

Upper Hot Springs Pool

Lake Minnewanka

Banff's lovely alpine setting, fine restaurants and sophisticated shopping make it an ideal combination of nature and culture. Within ten square kilometres alone (6 miles), visitors can rent a boat on Lake Minnewanka, go horseback riding in Sundance Canyon, discover the magnificent Banff Springs Hotel and enjoy a soak in the Upper Hot Springs Pool.

To make a tour of the townsite

Cascade Mountain and Banff Avenue

more interesting, visitors can rent a western-style horse and carriage. The path along the Bow River, where elk often graze, or the Fenland Trail on the outskirts of town also make for interesting excursions.

Because of the diverse range of activities which Banff has to offer, the area attracts outdoor lovers from all over the world.

Banff Springs Hotel

Banff Springs Hotel in the Winter

Banff Avenue

Bow Valley and the Bow River

Hoodoos

Bighorn Ram

Three Sisters

BOW VALLEY PARKWAY

Also known as the 1A Highway, this gently winding road is a quieter and a more leisurely alternative to the TransCanada Highway. Visitors journeying west to Lake Louise and beyond are more likely to see bears browsing for berries at the roadside if they choose this route.

Also on the Bow Valley Parkway is the interpretive trail which leads to Johnston Canyon. A pathway constructed between the canyon walls affords the visitor a spectacular view of a number of waterfalls.

Johnston Canyon

Moraine Lake and the Valley of the Ten Peaks

MORAINE LAKE

M oraine Lake is nestled in the Valley of the Ten Peaks. The peaks were originally named after the Stoney words for the numbers one through ten. Because the word for "ten" is "Wenkchemna," the valley has since been given this name.

A number of hiking trails branch out from Moraine Lake, near which the larches turn a lovely yellow color in autumn. Because this area compels visitors to linger, picnic tables accommodate those who may wish to enjoy their lunches out-doors.

Moraine Lake

Mt. Temple

Poppies

LAKE LOUISE

The Icelandic poppies which thrive on the shores of Lake Louise in the summer are well-suited to the glacier-cooled air circulating from the Plain of Six Glaciers above.

The trail along the lake leads either to the tea house below the glaciers or to the Lake Agnes tea house. These rustic cabins are a welcome sight for the hiker, as their

Lake Louise and the Lakeshore Trail

friendly staff serves simple but hearty meals.

The Chateau Lake Louise was originally built to attract visitors to the Rockies after the completion of the Canadian Pacific Railway. In 1890, it was merely a wooden chalet on the shore. Today, it houses 1000 guests who enjoy fine dining, elegant shops and a wonderful view of what the Stoneys described to early mountaineers as "the big snow mountain above the lake of little fishes."

Lake Louise and Victoria Glacier

Chateau Lake Louise

Lake Louise sunrise

Lake Agnes

Takakkaw Falls in Yoho Valley

Emerald Lake

YOHO

Natural Bridge, Kicking Horse River

The emblem of Yoho National Park is Takakkaw Falls. This cascade is aptly named, for in Cree, the word means "it is magnificent." From the trailhead at the falls, a path leads to Twin Falls and the tea house below.

En route to Takakkaw Falls is "the Meeting of the Waters," a popular viewpoint located where the Kicking Horse River meets the Yoho River. Because of the amount of spray generated at this turbulent junction, the vegetation which grows on the river bank is identical to the composition of the rain forests of the west coast.

Crowfoot Glacier

ICEFIELD PARKWAY

The Athabasca Glacier is one of eight outlet valley glaciers flowing down from the Columbia Icefield. Because of its close proximity to both the Icefield Parkway and the Forefield Trail, it is the most accessible glacier in North America.

An interesting way to discover the icefield is via Brewster Snocoach Tour, a vehicle which leads visitors directly onto the glacier where they can explore the mysterious landscape.

Bow Lake

Peyto Lake

Mount Chephren, Icefield Parkway

Icefield Parkway

Brewster Snocoach Tour, Icefield Parkway

Athabasca Falls

Sunwapta Falls

Maligne Lake

JASPER

Maligne Canyon

Maligne Lake derives its name from the curse of a Belgian missionary who, in the nineteenth century, had trouble crossing the river at its mouth. The canyon, which the river has carved over the course of 11,000 years, is the deepest and widest of all the limestone canyons in the Rockies.

No trip to Jasper is complete without a ride on the Jasper Tramway, which carries the visitor above montane, subalpine and alpine ecoregions, and affords a lovely view of the Athabasca and Miette River valleys.

Jasper Tramway

Jasper Park Lodge

Mount Edith Cavell

Mount Robson Provincial Park, British Columbia